Ho

Gareth Bird

www.gig-getter.com

What the music press say about Gig-Getter:

"Top Gig-Getting tips...you'll be playing more shows in no time" - **Total Guitar**

"Full of useful tips on how to organise and sell your band to promoters and press.....consider it a wake-up call" – **Guitar & Bass Magazine**

"Covers everything from finding potential venues then successfully approaching them....to keeping venues sold so they book you time after time......readers will be able to steal a march on their rivals" – **Performing Musician**

"Excellent" – **Bass Guitar**

"Feels like a labour of love, written by someone with genuine experience....filled with advice and ideas on how to market your band" – **Guitar Buyer**

"Get more gigs with Gig-Getter.....informative and practical steps to help any band get all the gigs they desire" – **Guitar Techniques**

"A fresh perspective...impressed me a great deal" - **Play Music**

"Fantastic!...it's about time someone did this" - **Play Pick-up Magazine**

Some reader feedback about Gig-Getter:

"I thought that I should finally write and just let you know how useful I have found your book. The responsibility for getting gigs has fallen to me (because if it was left to the others we'd never play!) and I didn't really have a clue about how to go about it. Your book helped to give me a lot of confidence, particularly around phoning venues to try and get gigs. Despite only having been gigging for 4 months we now have regular work...- I guess you do know what you're talking about!" – **Nick H. Exeter**

"An excellent book...valuable information"
– **Michael A. Richmond, Virginia**

"Your points and method all make perfect sense...you've given me a lot more confidence" - **Maurie B. Queensland**

"Packed with useful advice...thanks for writing the book"
– **Kim W. Topsham**

"Great tips and information" - **James G. London**

"A sort of Bible" – **Chris G. Glasgow**

"Invaluable information. Would benefit even the most established acts. A must read for any band looking for gigs"
- **Shane S. Dublin, Ireland**

"The coming year is looking even better.... we have 24 gigs already booked in with more promised that we have to fit in during the first half and at least another 8 for the second half. Our three gigs a month target is being ignored at the moment! Thanks for all your help and for the excellent book".
- Clive M. Warwick

"Best I've read on the subject" – **Simon C. Cardiff**

"I really recommend Gig-Getter" - **Karl D. Leeds**

"I just wanted to drop you a line to thank you for your excellent book.... just by getting ourselves a little more organised and doing a little research (on venues and other bands in the area) we suddenly find that we are booked up to play throughout every weekend in June !!!

Being based in Cambridge there are a great many student type bands in the area and the city centre venues cater mainly for that audience. As an aged 40+ band (i.e. old enough to know better!), we found it a struggle to get bookings.........

All the best and thanks again for a great book"
– **Paul K. Cambridge (5 days after receiving his copy of Gig-Getter)**

CONTENTS

Introduction

Part One: *Getting ready to market your band*

1. Working out what's different about your band   11
   - Treat it like a business
   - You too can sell your band
   - Check out your competition
   - Understand your own strengths & weaknesses
   - Discover your uniqueness (USP)
   - Improve on what you've got

2. Polishing up your act – How to make sure you're good enough   19
   - What are you going to play?
   - Who is your audience?
   - Practise really does make perfect
   - Ok, so how do you look?
   - Open Mic nights
   - Audience feedback

3. How many gigs can you handle?   25
   - Set yourself gig-getting goals
   - How much time have you got?
   - What are you worth?
   - Decide who's in charge of the gig diary

4. Taking aim - Where do you find venues?   29
   - Other band's websites
   - Newspapers
   - Venue notice boards/word of mouth
   - Festivals & fairs
   - Hotels
   - Weddings & private functions
   - Your own gigs

Part Two: _Going for it – Marketing your band from a standing start_

5. How to keep track of all your bookings   35
   - The gig-getter's diary
   - Other commitments

6. Organising your ongoing gig-getting efforts   39
   - Set yourself apart from other acts
   - The Gig-getter organiser

7. How to create a demo that gets listened to   43
   - Why do you need a demo?
   - Live or studio?
   - The 5 minute medley
   - Which songs should you record?
   - Recording the demo
   - Editing your demo
   - Your final product
   - What more could they want?

8. How to easily get gigs over the phone   51
    -   How to make yourself feel confident about the call
    -   The simple call for information - the 1st call
    -   Seeing how you can help them - the 2nd call
    -   Your vital first words to the booker
    -   They're all ears: now what?
    -   Closing the deal and the call

9. What else can you do for the venue?   63
    -   Let people INSIDE the venue know
    -   Letting people OUTSIDE the venue know
    -   Getting the local press interested in you

Part Three: *Gig Night*

10. Creating a memorable live show every time   71
    -   Dress up or dress down?
    -   Let the "hirer" have input into what you play
    -   Rent-a-crowd
    -   Your set list(s)
    -   Dealing with audience requests
    -   Getting the audience involved
    -   What to do if "disaster" strikes

11. Advertising while you play   79
    -   Get your name in front of the whole audience
    -   Make your name known

12. Take photos   81
    -   Don't forget your audience
    -   Include ALL the band
    -   Don't let your wardrobe let you down
    -   Use venue "landmarks"

13. Use what people say — 85
    - The power of praise
    - What do you do with the quotation?
    - How to use quotations to sell your band

14. How to make sure you get paid & more bookings — 89
    - Show me the money
    - Strike while the iron's still red-hot

Part Four: Onwards & upwards

15. The easy way to fill your gig diary — 95
    - Repeat work at the same venue

16. More ways you can use the press — 97
    - Establish your target publications
    - Send out regular press releases
    - What do the press want to know?

17. How to get venues to CALL YOU — 103
    - Stay in touch
    - Create your newsletter
    - Following up

A final word from me to you — 109

Gig-Getter timetable — 111

Index

INTRODUCTION

So you've got your band and your material together – Now what?

Congratulations! This is the time and place for you to take all your learning and rehearsing and turn it into a new way of life, playing as often as you like in front of other people for money. A new way of life that can give you the creative outlet, admiration and satisfaction that you've only ever dreamt of through your music. In this manual, you're going to be given my own proven step-by-step guide for starting out with little more than a few songs and a desire to play them, to making a good second income as a semi-pro entertainer. None of these steps are difficult to understand and they don't require any skill to carry them out.

One or two of the techniques I'll give you might seem obvious when you first hear them but most will not. Each step will demonstrate a different, successful gig-getting approach. A number of these approaches or a combination of them, are bound to be right for your current situation too.

You should understand though, right at the start, what this manual is *not*. It is *not* just another book of general ideas about how to "make it big" in the music business or about getting a record deal. Nor is it about how to form a band or write songs. If you need to learn how to put lyrics together, play your instrument better or get together with other musicians - there are countless books and websites out there that can teach you those things. I don't see any reason to write yet another one.

Getting all the gigs you want needn't involve a lot of time, expense or sacrifice.

This is *not* the kind of book that recommends you spend a fortune (or anything at all for that matter), advertising your act. Nor do I believe that you have to work every hour God sends trying to sell your band to other people in order to get gigs. You don't need to perform for free and your day job, studies or social & family lives certainly don't have to suffer in order for you to succeed in creating a following for your act. Most of the performers I meet who pay money to promote their band or who play for nothing, do so because they feel they can't get gigs any other way or because their shows are as dull as dish water, or in my experience, they're playing for no fees because they're scared they're not really worth being paid.

I've never really understood how performing music can be thought of as enjoyable if it doesn't improve things like your social life, bank balance and your overall happiness. A working semi-pro music act, if you run it the way I'm going to show you, will significantly improve your lifestyle in terms of the numbers of people you'll get to know, your own personal happiness & satisfaction, your income and your musical creativity. Hopefully, this manual will demonstrate to you that you can have a very successful 2nd career as a performer AND a life at the same time.

Don't you wish people who are all theory would stop giving advice?

Although this is a "How to" guide about turning your musical talent and experience into a successful live act, it is *not* a book of theory. I don't know about you, but I've never had much time for gig-getting guides made up of out of date ideas written by slipper-wearing strummers who gave up playing years ago. I'm asked a lot about how I manage to get my band out as often as I do and with as much prestigious work as we get. I always warn any enquirer about other writers whose experience in getting gigs is only a distant memory. I live and play in the here and now, where we're all only as good as our last performance. So I'll give you an honest guarantee; every one of the methods and steps that I share with you in this manual will be one that I have real personal experience with getting gigs for my band. They are all approaches that I've used myself and they have been repeatedly proven to succeed and continue to do so.

What price do you put on playing regularly at places like the Hard Rock Cafe?

All of the information in this manual has come from my own experience and my gig-getting work. You may be interested to know that more than 80% of the places we play immediately book us to come back and play again. The bulk of the ones which don't, do so at a later date. My band are regulars at one of the world's most instantly recognised rock venues – the Hard Rock Café. Recently I took my other half to our nearest Café for a meal on her birthday. The manager (who's responsible for booking the bands) came over and sat with us. He refused to let me pay for our meals. Now I'm not particularly interested in the money I saved, but more what it says about the impression my band has made on a place like that.

More importantly, last week they called me at home to arrange a string of bookings for my band right through to the end of next year.

Please don't think I'm telling you any of this to try and make myself sound great. When I first decided to use what I knew about selling and see if it could be applied to getting-gigs, I said to myself that if I could succeed, I would try to help other frustrated part-time musicians get their acts out of the bedroom and onto the stage, the same as me. That's what I'm trying to do here. I need you to know the value of what you're going to read in the following pages. It's a lot more than the price you paid for the manual. At the very least it's worth the same sort of amount as just one of the lowest-paying kind of bar or pub gigs would pay you, say £200. This manual stands for hundreds of £'s worth of mistakes, thousands of £'s of successful gigs and greater satisfaction as a performing musician than I ever dreamt possible, when I first picked up my bass guitar only a few years ago.

Try to keep all this in mind, because what you get out of Gig-Getter will be directly influenced by the value you believe it has.

Finally, in this manual, you will find a total of seventeen steps covering different methods to aid your gig-getting success. I recommend you read these steps and apply them in the order you find them. This way I guarantee you'll get the most benefit from Gig-Getter. If you later feel you need to concentrate more on any one particular step then you can obviously refer back to it.

So, let's get started...

PART ONE: **Getting ready to market your band**

1. Working out what's different about your band

2. Polishing up your act – How to make sure you're good enough

3. How many gigs can you handle?

4. Taking aim - Where do you find venues?

Step 1: Working out what's different about your band

1.1 Treat it like a business

The big secret which will make the greatest difference to your success or failure in gaining and keeping gigs is simple. Treat your act like a business. Even when no-one has ever paid you a penny to perform.

This doesn't mean you have to get all serious and spoil the idea of the band being fun. All I'm talking about is getting a little organised in your efforts to promote yourself. Then you can just watch the work pile in.

1.2 You too can sell your band

The idea of "promoting" yourself, of "selling" can strike fear into the hearts of many people. We artists and performers can be sensitive souls who either feel it's beneath them to get out there and push themselves or feel very uncomfortable doing it.

Selling in the traditional sense has got itself a bit of a bad press. The good news though is that it's not the foot-in-the-door, pestering kind of face to face activity you may associate with selling that you'll need here.

Gig-getting without an agent is more of a gentle process, of letting the person who books acts for any particular venue know that you exist, and giving them reasons why they should book you.

As you'll see, you do this in a simple yet very effective step-by-step manner in a way which can't offend anyone and

11

which will give even the shyest performer very little (if any) stress or discomfort.

1.3 <u>Check out your competition</u>

This is the big difference between scratching round trying to get a few gigs and in running it like a business. You have to do the preparation first before you start to promote your band. You have to understand exactly what it is you're offering and why people should hire you.

The first step in this applies whether you're a seasoned performer who just wants more work or someone who's never played their guitar away from the bedroom mirror. Once you know what sort of act you want to perform (i.e. rock covers/indie/country or whatever) you have to find out who else locally is doing what you do. We'll look later at checking out the acts who are playing at the venues you have in mind (no matter what sort of music the acts are). For now though, let's just focus on other bands who play the kind of things you do or intend to do. For example, if you've established a heavy metal band playing original material you need to find out which other original metal bands are gigging in your area.

You can do this via two main routes:
    a) Website searches
    b) Venue advertisements

a) Website searches

This is the key which opened a lot of doors for me when I first got my band started on the road to plentiful regular gigs. I did a Google search on rock covers bands in my area. When I saw the websites it brought up, I clicked in and explored them. There were only a couple but they were both a goldmine of information for me.

12

They told me:

- What the bands considered unique about themselves
- Where the bands played
- What the bands played (i.e. the song titles)
- The quality of the bands (via MP3 clips)

This information will prove priceless as we go forward, as soon you'll see.

b) <u>Venue advertisements</u>
This assumes you know some local venues that have live acts on. If not, you need to find venues by:

- Keeping your eyes open for pub and club notice boards while you're round the shops or in town
- Checking the entertainment section of the local paper
- Study the notice board at local music shops
- Read the music press gig listings
- Web searches for venue sites ("live music/gigs/ venues in Boston")

Ideally, once you identify the competition you should make an effort to go and watch them. Check some of the venues you'd like to be playing at and the quality level you'll need to reach when you do. Watching your competition live will give you clearer ideas on what they're good at but also show what they're poor at (great singer but mediocre lead guitarist perhaps). One important point here: Don't let yourself be overawed or dismayed if your competition seems too good for you to match if and when you watch them. There will be things they're not so good at if you keep looking. Perhaps they weren't good at relaxing the audience with a little banter in between some of the numbers. Or maybe, despite their technical "brilliance", the choice of material didn't quite do it for the audience? Either way this is all information which will help you when we start to examine your own act before trying to sell it.

1.4 Understand your own strengths & weaknesses

Remember, you're still only doing this for your own understanding at this point. Once you have some idea of what else is out there you'll be in better shape to look at the features of your own act. You need to be able to compare and contrast the various parts of your band, with what you've learned of others.

The easiest place to start is by listing down all the features of your band. Just the facts to start with like:

- Numbers of people in the band
- Instruments played
- Band and individual members musical history
- Ages
- Where you're based
- Where (if anywhere) you've played before
- Type of material etc.

Once you've thought of as many of the <u>facts</u> relating to your band as you can, you need to ask yourself: What are the best and worst features of your band or act? You've got to be honest with yourself here. If you're balding and have a beer gut, list that down. It's a fact. If you have any experience of live work then you may well have invaluable audience comments to draw on in terms of your best and worst aspects. If not, you might consider letting a friend or partner listen to you and watch you rehearse so you can get some feedback on what you do.

Let me give you some examples of what I established about my band when I did this exercise.

Some weaknesses:
- *Inexperienced/rudimentary bassist.* (Me, basically. I'd only been playing a couple of years and was still only learning how to do any more than the root notes)
- *Band member's ages:* With two of us greying and in our 40's we weren't exactly liable to appeal to younger audiences.
- *Stage "act".* With the exception of the lead singer, the band did little more on stage than stare at their instruments/the floor while standing (or sitting in the drummer's case) rooted to the spot.

Some strengths:
- *Lead singer's interaction with the crowd.* Although perhaps not technically the greatest vocalist for the rock covers we had chosen to focus on, our singer was good at establishing some sort of rapport with an audience. Nothing clever really, just some comments and a little banter in between numbers but still much more than many acts we'd watched.
- *Lead Guitarist.* Perhaps because his appearance as one of the "greys" mentioned above, but his ability to copy note for note any lead break he played and with great feel, was a source of admiration amongst band and audience members.
- *Width of material.* We had learned more than 2 sets worth of material spanning almost 5 decades. We could offer material that any age group would at least recognise. (This had to increase our chances of being hired. We'll look at that later).

1.5 <u>Discover your uniqueness (USP)</u>

Sales & marketing people often talk about the USP of their product. This sounds technical but actually just stands for "Unique Selling Point(s)".

In our case all it means is this:

What's different / unique about our band? What sets us apart from other bands of the same type?

You find this out during the process above (studying your competition and looking at your strengths and weaknesses). Generally it's a combination of the most important things you uncover in that process. It's something you should be able to condense into a one liner.

For example, my current band's USP would be that we offer venues:

"A wide range of pop and rock covers from a fairly good-looking band with great audience interaction and a track record (now) of playing at a number of prestigious venues in the area"

1.6 <u>Improve on what you've got.</u>

Of course it's possible that what you find out about yourself or your act isn't unique in any way, or in enough of a way. If that really is the case, and you've asked other people who've seen you, you'll need to do something about it. The most obvious approach would be to look at each of the weaknesses you uncovered and ask yourself how you could turn it into a positive. Could the average drummer improve or be replaced by someone significantly better? Could your introverted singer be helped out by the more sociable keyboard player taking over with some well-rehearsed banter with the audience between songs? Should the narrow appeal of your original metal material be widened with the inclusion of a few standard rock classics?

You get the idea.

The first step is done. You've worked out what's different about your act. Now you need to focus on making sure you're good enough when you start playing all these extra gigs.

Working out what's different about your band

Step 2: **Polishing up your act – How to make sure you're good enough**

2.1 <u>What are you going to play?</u>

The first thing you might want to think about here is that you're likely to get a lot more work if you're playing covers and not just your own original material. Venues which cater to acts performing their own songs are limited, whilst it's no exaggeration to say that there are a number of venues for covers acts in every town.

My advice, if you're really determined to play your own material, would be to mix some of your own numbers in with the covers. At least in the beginning, to build a following and gain exposure. Think about it. Many big name bands have at some point included at least a cover or two. From your point of view, most audiences do like to hear what they already know and this way you can keep everyone happy and showcase your own songs (even sell CDs at the gig if there's enough audience enthusiasm).

2.2 <u>Who is your audience?</u>

Think about the typical person who goes to the type of venues you play or would like to play at. What are they into? What ages are they? If, for example, you like the idea of playing weddings (these can be VERY lucrative) then you'll need to compile sets of songs which appeal to a wide age group. Personally, I'd advise on this approach anyway because inevitably the more people you appeal to the more work you'll get.

This doesn't mean you have to compromise your musical values. If you search, you should be able to find and adapt crowd pleasing covers from any decade from the 50's onwards.

From the 50's for example – Elvis, the 60's maybe the Kinks and Beatles, 70's everything from T.Rex through to Free and the Sex Pistols. Use your imagination and something like the Guinness Book of Hit Singles.

If this sounds like "selling out" to you and you're not prepared to compromise on your own particular fetish for Thrash Metal that's ok. Just know that there will be less gigs available to you and you'll have to work that much harder to fill your gig diary yourself if you choose that avenue.

2.3 **Practise really does make perfect**

Once you've chosen your material, you'll need to rehearse it until you can play it almost without thinking. This is particularly true if you suffer from performance nerves. The more often you practise something, the easier it becomes. Almost to the point of being able to play or sing things in your sleep (or under the influence). If getting everyone together to rehearse isn't always possible and you're a guitarist or bassist, you might want to try the *Tascam* Guitar or Bass Trainer. This small piece of kit allows you to play MP3's (CD's on the older version), and to mute your part so you can play along as if practising with the band. You can also slow the tempo for those tricky parts until you've fully mastered them. *Boss* also do something similar.

Either way, even before you have a steady supply of gigs coming in, you should schedule a weekly session to run through your material and later to add in new material in between gigs.

As you develop and become more active on the gig circuit, you'll also want to rehearse to make changes to certain aspects of some of your established numbers. Perhaps to create a more interesting ending for a number, or to iron out any particularly tricky parts that you have trouble with in a live situation.

2.4 <u>Ok, so how do you look?</u>

As well as knowing your material inside out before you set foot on stage, there's another aspect to consider before you start trying to seriously increase your number of performances. You need to perfect your look as well as your sound.

You'll have to try and take an honest look at yourself to start with. It's one thing to be a long haired 18 year old wanting to play your own Nirvana-inspired material. But what if you're a balding pot bellied 45 year old who needs to strut his stuff?

You don't need to worry that people will judge you negatively for the way you look. In my experience it can actually be an asset if you don't look like the kind of person who "should" be playing exciting music. I've known crew-cut white haired guitarists in their 50's shuffle onto a stage in baggy jeans and rip out wonderful lead breaks to the delight of the audience. The point is that those white or grey haired members of the audience can readily identify with performers like that in a way that they couldn't with a younger, more "typical muso".

You can of course make sure you look reasonably trendy but in a way which suits your physical appearance. In simple terms, you won't go far wrong with a t-shirt and jeans. You can use different jean styles for different classes of venues (I use black for weddings). The t-shirt is a perfect device for making a statement about your "attitude" through whatever motif is displayed on the clothing in question.

For example, if I play a bikers pub (which I have on a number of occasions), its ripped jeans and a scruffy black shirt.

Jeans and t-shirts enable you to fit in and dress suitably for most venues. Depending on the type of music you're playing and the venues you're targeting, there may be the odd time when a more formal shirt is required. Keep it plain and simple. Black is good to hide any excess bulk while still looking stylish and avoids being "cheesy". Unless of course, cheese is the look you're after.

2.5 <u>Open Mic nights</u>
When you have your material and your look but no gigs, what can you do to get some experience? Keep an eye out for the many Open Mic nights you will see around. These involve a kind of free for all where any musician and/or singer can get up and do a turn in front of a largely supportive audience of others. Experience of getting up in front of other people is all you're looking for here.

2.6 <u>Audience feedback</u>
The final point about making sure you're good enough relates more to when you are performing. You should continually try to improve your performances. Your audiences can often provide you with very useful information. To ensure you get some feedback, encourage your partner or friends who are watching to give their <u>honest</u> opinions. Later, your "groupies" (or followers before you get to the stage of having "groupies") may offer their feedback.

Don't be afraid of asking them which numbers in particular they thought worked well and which didn't. Which were their favourites? Are there any other aspects of the performance that could be improved?

In the early days of my current band we had a problem with lengthy gaps in between numbers. This was fed back to us a number of times by various people so we finally addressed it by looking for ways one instrument could start a particular song alone, almost as soon as the preceding number had finished. That way we could keep the momentum going if the moment called for it.

If you listen to what people tell you about your performances, and if you gauge their responses on the night (i.e. which numbers or which comments your front man makes go down best) you'll be able to adjust the content of what you do as you go forward. Then you'll be giving people more of what they want. This is the secret to successfully satisfying your audiences and ultimately getting asked back by the venue.

By now you should have made sure you're up to the job of entertaining your audience and satisfying the person who hires you once you're up there on the stage.

You now have an important consideration before you start getting gigs. Everyone involved in your band needs to agree just how often you want to get out and perform.

Polishing up your act – How to make sure you're good enough

Step 3: How many gigs can you handle?

3.1 Set yourself gig-getting goals

When we come to look at the nuts and bolts of gig-getting shortly, you'll learn that the amount of time you can play a month will depend on 5 things:

a) How much time you have available to get out and play
b) How much you charge
c) How many venues you're talking to
d) What you say when you contact these venues
e) How well their audiences respond to you

We'll cover all of the above as we go through this manual but in particular in this step we need to consider the first two points above. Firstly, your available time and then while still at this planning stage you need to consider and agree between you how much you are happy with charging any venue.

3.2 How much time have you got?

It's crucial that you agree between you (assuming you're not a solo artist), exactly what you're all happy with. In the past I've been accused of bringing in too many gigs per month (yes, this can happen), and asked to slow things down a little. When this involves cancelling work it can be both embarrassing for you and it really doesn't shed a good light on you as reliable performers.

We all have other commitments besides our music, whether it's a full-time day job, a family or our studies. These may

25

well be different for each band member and between you you'll have to reach an agreement on frequency of playing.

So, everyone concerned should agree on limits of gigs you want to handle per month. Then you, as the prime gig-getter, shouldn't exceed these.

Limited availability can actually be something of an attraction for a venue. They don't need to know that you only want to work 2 weekend nights per month, for example. So when you have your nights sorted out for any month you're "fully booked". To the venue booker this will suggest a successful band that's in demand. An important side-benefit, along with keeping all the band members (not to mention their wives/partners) happy.

3.3 **What are you worth?**
What you can charge will vary a little from venue to venue, considerably from region to region and a lot between types of functions and venues. Some bar work can offer as little as £150, where as weddings and corporate work can pay you in excess of £1,000. Obviously we'd all like to get £1,000 or more every time we play. But how many of us can guarantee that enough well-paying event organisers know of our existence?

In simple terms, the less you charge the more often you can be gigging. Some venues will have small budgets and so will have fewer reasons not to book you if your price isn't an issue. These venues can be used to build your track record.

Am I recommending you go out for next to nothing? No, but you do need to build a track record. For example, we went out for less money every weekend when we were starting than we'd consider now. This enabled us to build valuable gigging experience and something approaching a following. You might like to think of early low-paying gigs as a means to an end. A platform to get you in front of as many people as possible.

At this stage you just need an idea of what you'll all be happy going out for. You'll be able to refine your expectations as you start to talk to venues. Two things to bear in mind here:

a) Quoting too low a price can make venues think you can't be any good

b) It can pay to offer a reduced "Trial Price" to venues on the understanding that this will be reviewed for further gigs.

3.4 Decide who's in charge of the gig diary

In order to make sure your future gig-getting efforts avoid confusion or even chaos, I would advise you to appoint one person only as the "keeper" of the band's gig-diary (see Step 5 in Part 2).

That person (you, presumably) will be conducting the pro-active step-by-step approach to gig getting explained in the next section. However, any band member can take a booking should they receive an approach or find some venue (perhaps local to them) that they want to approach for themselves. This should be agreed beforehand so that you don't have 2 band members approaching the same venue. You can imagine how that would look to the place concerned...

I would advise you, as the gig-getter, to make sure that every approach is channelled through you (i.e. you know promptly about any approaches made by other band members). Then you can make sure you're sticking to the agreed frequency of gigs you established earlier. It's pointless you merrily charging on with bookings for 2 months time if other band members have already filled every available slot. Later in the manual (Step 5) I'll show you a suggested gig-getting diary which you can use to communicate between band members to avoid any problems or confusion.

So you know the basics to consider before you begin selling and getting your band booked. Now you need someone to sell to, someone who will hire your act.

Step 4: Taking aim- Where do you find venues?

Before you even begin looking for venues to approach it's vital, like in any kind of selling, to get yourself in the right frame of mind. You need to focus yourself on trying to help the venue out. You don't (just) want to get your hand in their pocket and take their money and you don't want to push your band onto them. You're going to be in the business of **solving their entertainment problems**.

First you need to identify the right kind of venues for your band. Once you've found a venue, check to find out the type of music they feature. If you're unsure, a simple phone call to the place as if you're an "interested punter" can be all you need. Ask whether they ever have "Country & Western" (if that's what you do) acts on.

So where do you look?

4.1 Other band's websites

Remember that work we did earlier where we looked at your competition and your own strengths and weaknesses? If you used other band's websites in this process, you have a ready made font of useful gig sourcing. Just look in the "gig info" section of their website and check out the names of forthcoming (and past) places they've played.

Some bands will go to the trouble of giving their website visitors a telephone number for the venue in question! Perfect. So go through these websites and jot down anything you can about the venues they've played at. If there are no contact details or you're not familiar with any of them, a simple Google search will, 9 times out of 10, reveal their address and contact details.

4.2 Newspapers

I've had plenty of work for my band from contacting venues who have placed ads about forthcoming live bands/acts in the local press. The key is to make sure that each band member browses their own local evening paper for likely targets. The more the merrier.

4.3 Venue notice boards/word of mouth

This, again, is just a question of keeping your eyes and ears open while out and about. If you see notice boards up outside pubs or clubs advertising live nights, then add that venue to your target list. Similarly if someone mentions they saw a band somewhere, you need details, so that venue too can be added to your targets.

4.4 Festivals & fairs

As well as places that regularly have live music (the easiest places to target first for your band), anywhere that has some form of music entertainment (i.e. a D.J.) is fair game. We've gained some lucrative work through persuading local PTA organisers to give the kids the thrill of seeing a live band in the flesh and have us on at their summer fetes (for a fee of course). If you have kids at school (or you know someone who does) get these people on your list.

4.5 Hotels

Hotels can be well-paid places to play and if your local ones are part of a well-known chain they can add great credibility to your band's "C.V.". Many of them have function rooms and you can get yourself on to their "Wedding entertainment" list which they will make available to couples who book their wedding at the hotel concerned and who may want live entertainment.

In addition though, many hotels tend to be very quiet at weekends when the usual business people aren't around. I've used this fact to secure regular work at prestigious hotels in order to help them bring additional drinkers into their otherwise empty bar areas. So, list down any local hotels you and the other band members may have.

4.6 <u>Weddings & private functions</u>

In addition to weddings and other private parties which can come your way if a hotel is aware of you, you should always be on the look out for private bookings yourself. If you know someone who's getting married, turning 30 or whatever, maybe they would consider a live band as part of the entertainment? You might be surprised at how much of this work you can get (and the size of the fees involved) particularly when your name becomes known locally.

Much of this kind of work will come your way as a direct result of playing other types of gigs (pubs, clubs etc) which is why you'll hear me talk about advertising your name at gigs later on.

4.7 <u>Your own gigs</u>

If all else fails you can always organise something yourself. This can take the form of a glorified party where you invite all the band members' family and friends. Remember, make sure they bring their own alcohol (and some for the band if you're not charging them entry) if the venue doesn't have a bar.

What you're after here is:

a) Exposure, where people can see you perform and subsequently book you for a function of some kind.
b) Experience of playing in front of other people.

If this doesn't sound like your thing, remember that **the more people who see you the more chance you have of getting booked to play again elsewhere.** Like many things in selling it's just a numbers game. If you stay at home strumming in the bedroom the world will never know.

So, now we've done all the preparation needed. You've worked out what's unique about your act; you've rehearsed and sorted out your look. You even have your list of potential venues. What now?

You need to get out there and market your band. Here's how.

PART TWO: **Going for it - Marketing your band from a standing start**

5.   How to keep track of all your bookings

6.   Organising your ongoing gig-getting efforts

7.   How to create a demo that gets listened to

8.   How to easily get gigs over the phone

9.   What else can you do for the venue?

Step 5: How to keep track of all your bookings

So you've done all the preparation you need. Now to book your act out.

5.1 The gig-getter's diary

The key tool to making sure you properly organise your availability for future gigs and don't double-book yourself is a shared diary, something that each member of the band can have a continually updated copy of.

Ideally, you'll email this between the group of you each time it's updated with another booking. You'll also keep it in front of you as part of your tool-kit when you're on the phone to venues. It's something that, as time goes by, you as the gig getter should have with you at all times.

Why? Well, once you become active in getting your name and availability around, venues will call <u>you</u> to see whether you're available on certain nights.

You might say to yourself:

"What difference does it make? I can always call them back when I've checked the diary to see if we're available when they want us".

True enough, but I've discovered some venues initially put you on a reserve list and will call you when an act they currently use let's them down for a particular date. At this point the venue manager goes down his list calling each of those bands on his "reserve" until he finds one who's available. Its first come first served in those circumstances so you can see the benefit of being armed with your gig diary (and mobile phone) as often as you can.

5.2 <u>Other commitments</u>

When you first put your gig diary together for the year, get each band member to fill out any particular nights they're unavailable through other commitments, when they're away with holidays etc. Everyone has to agree to keep the nominated gig-getter (i.e. you) updated on any new commitments that may occur ASAP. There's nothing more likely to undermine a venues confidence in the reliability of a new act, than you having to try and rearrange a booking before you've even played for them.

On the next page I've included a layout of the simple universal gig diary my band uses between ourselves to co-ordinate our activities. Feel free to copy this and use it yourself. You can put the name of the days in for whatever year your working on and highlight (via colour-coded shading) the weekends - your prime targets for gigs. Also, highlight when band members are unavailable. You'll then be able to keep on top of your gig-getting efforts at a glance. Alternatively, Google offer a great free online calendar that is available via their search engine (www.google.com/calendar).

Once you have available dates from the other members and you've already agreed how many bookings a month you want to limit yourselves to, you'll know exactly what you're aiming for. The goals will be to fill those dates that are actually free.

Gig Getter Diary

	Jan	Feb	Mar	Apr	May	June	July	Aug	Sep	Oct	Nov	Dec
1												
2												
3												
4												
5												
6												
7												
8												
9												
10												
11												
12												
13												
14												
15												
16												
17												
18												
19												
20												
21												
22												
23												
24												
25												
26												
27												
28												
29												
30												
31												

How to keep track of all your bookings

Step 6: **Organising your ongoing gig-getting efforts**

Once we get to the telephone script stage in Step 8, you'll find you'll get some gigs during the very first phone call. Others may take a couple of contacts. Either way, you want to be well organised so you can see exactly where you're up to with any new or potential venue.

6.1 <u>Set yourself apart from other acts</u>

To do this you need to create a simple method of recording your efforts. This easy yet very effective way of keeping on top of things will also set you apart from other bands who are trying to get work for themselves. As you'll see, a system like the one I'll show you will let your professional attitude shine through. I know for a fact that this will feel like a breath of fresh air to the busy manager used to having to deal with faceless agents or disorganised amateurs.

What exactly do you need? If you want to get really sophisticated, and have access to one, then business development or CRM software such as ACT! is perfect. However, it's far from essential. A simple "spreadsheet" drawn up on one of the band member's computers is all you need. You'll want columns for the venue name, Manager/booker name and contact details and a series of other columns showing results and dates of each of your conversations with them and any follow-up action points.

Failing this, a simple paper and pen will be enough.

6.2 <u>Gig-getter organiser</u>

Page 41 shows you what one should look like. You can either copy it for yourself or adjust it if you want to try and improve it. Trust me though, in this format it's really all you need.

On the blank sheet there are spaces for just 9 venues. On my current contacts organiser list there are around 50 venues over 5 pages and I'd advise you to aim for a similar number as you progress. In case you're not sure, use the "table" tab at the top of the MS Word new document page then insert a table with 10 columns and a similar number of rows to get you started.

Using something like the example opposite means you can keep on top of things with a full record of discussions with each venue. Whenever and wherever you need to do something, highlight it in the action column. Your focus then should be on those columns containing the latest highlighted comments relating to the venue in question. This way you can see exactly what you need to do next to make a gig happen with that venue.

If you're using a PC to draw up your own organiser sheet, leave the size of the columns/rows so that they flex to the words that fit inside (auto fit to window). That way you'll be able to fit any amount of words you need into the relevant space. Clearly if you have a lot to say then you're not going to get many venues on the one sheet – but this is no big deal it just means you'll have more pages to deal with.

Now you have your working document which you update as you approach your list of venues. Next we're going to look at another key weapon for the gig-getter. This is something that you may not use that much once you get established but if you're starting out it's essential and often requested – your demo.

Organising your ongoing gig-getting efforts

Gig Getter Venue Contacts

Venue	Name/No.	Contact	Action	Contact	Action	Contact	Action	Contact	Action

Organising your ongoing gig-getting efforts

Step 7: How to create a demo that gets listened to

7.1 Why do you need a demo?
Once you start to get yourself a reputation as a live act or have a few well-known venues on your "CV" these things alone will be your calling card and will generate work for you. But before that time comes, you'll need some proof of what you can do. Call it a "sample" if you like. A brief taster of you playing.

7.2 Live or studio?
You may think you need to spend a fortune getting yourself into a studio to have a professional recording done. Rest assured this won't be necessary providing one of the band has some basic music editing software on his PC and a simple sound recorder.

You're trying to use your music demo to get live work, so to really convince your listener you need to record something which can be considered to be you playing live.

To do this and to give yourself a unique edge over submissions other acts might make, you shouldn't record any complete songs.

7.3 The 5 minute medley
Remember your work in Step 1 where you looked at your strengths and weaknesses and the uniqueness of your act? You're going to create a 5 minute medley of snatches of songs which best showcase these strengths.

One of the beauties of a 5 minute medley is that you don't need to try and record any audience reaction (clapping, cheering etc) as each song finishes. This would obviously be very difficult for you to achieve if you've never played anywhere significant. A medley also invites the listener to whiz through the whole CD as there are no natural pauses in it. That way he or she is far more likely to hear all that you want them to rather than just a part.

7.4 <u>Which songs should you record?</u>

If a wide range of material is one of your key points of difference, make sure you have a wide selection of tracks on the demo. Even if sweeping musical genres is not what you're about, you should try to introduce some variation through the recording. Don't use only upbeat tracks, add a couple of slower songs on there as well.

You need to keep in mind the key strengths you established earlier. For example, when creating our demo the first track we used was a number which highlighted the strength of both our backing vocals and our note perfect lead guitarist. That way we hit the listener immediately with some of our key strengths.

Remember, what you're looking to produce is a music sample different from the complete numbers that are usually found on a Myspace page, for example. We're creating something specifically aimed at getting you gigs.

On the finished product, you're looking for snippets of only 5 or 10 second bursts of music, but how do you produce this?

7.5 **Recording the demo**

The best way to go about recording your demo is to either:

a) Record each individual instrument separately into your PC music software.
b) If you have sufficiently high quality digital recording equipment – record yourself rehearsing.

If you're doing the latter, I recommend simply leaving the recorder on through a whole rehearsal session so you can use it all as raw material which you can then later transfer to your PC and edit.

Either way, decide in advance which numbers/sections of numbers you want to include on your demo and concentrate on these as you rehearse.

If you record a rehearsal and you're going through it later, you may find there are key parts (big lead break/keyboard solo etc) which haven't recorded as well as you'd like. These can be re-done at a later date when you fine tune what you have. Don't worry about not getting things perfect in one go. You'll probably find it will take you 3 or 4 sessions to get everything you want, so plan this early in your gig-getting efforts and give yourself plenty of time.

7.6 **Editing your demo**

Once you're happy with the basic content of the material you've recorded, you'll need to polish it up with EQ (equalisation) and compression etc. It's beyond the scope of this manual to go into any detail on that but if you're a real novice I recommend you start picking up something like "Computer Music" magazine. This will give you useful tips on recording and editing music. It also regularly gives away free music producing and editing software which you might find useful if money is an issue.

Assuming you have some idea about editing to get the sound you want, what you're looking to produce is a total of 5 minutes made up of several snippets of music. You'll then weave these into one medley. Make sure there's some variation in place and show off as many of your playing "highlights" as you can as we looked at earlier.

I'd recommend starting and finishing the demo with clips from the same number (both showcasing different parts of the song/different elements of your playing). This will give a good balance to the demo. For the ending, if you have a suitable number with a big ending, use that. If not, simply fade it out using your software.

7.7 <u>Your final product</u>

We've produced 2 demos over the 3 years we've been together. (The first featured a keyboard player who left, meaning we had to update our demo as a new 4-piece without the ivory-tinkling). The first was a CD produced using an expensive copying service that also printed a picture and details onto the CD itself and made a sleeve.

Time and technology have moved on and you can now do the same thing from your own PC for very little money. You'll need a photo printer which can print the face of blank white CDs and some software such as *MediaFace*. The software will help you design the look of the CD. If you don't own a printer which can produce pictures on the CD itself – or have access to one, there are plenty of printing companies who can do this for you. Check your local directories and the music press for ideas.

Whichever way you do it, you'll save yourself some money and effort by doing what we did on our 2nd and final CD.

Forget the CD cover/sleeve. ***Get all the information you need to get across onto the CD itself.***

What exactly should you put on the CD or make accessible with the MP3 (if your demo's in that format) for maximum effect?

a) <u>Background picture</u>
This should be consistent with the type of music you play. For example if your material is Sinatra & Andy Williams covers you'll probably want something like a standard portrait shot of you or the band. A band with attitude might prefer a moody full-length pose by the band or (as in our case) a picture taken live.

We'll be looking in Step 12 at how to build up a good portfolio of band pictures but know now that if you compose the picture well, it will go a long way to selling what you're about. For me, the ideal picture to aim for when you can, is you playing live which also includes in-shot, some positive audience reaction.

b) <u>Genre & list of your material</u>
You want to make it easy for the venue to classify what you do. It can happen that the person who receives your demo needs to convince a partner or boss about you or possibly the venue booker changes and the demo gets handed on. You'll need your demo to be able to sell itself even before it's been listened to, rather than rely on someone else to try and do that for you. Remember, you may be targeting hotels for corporate or wedding work and the event planners at the hotels will need to understand (and remember) what you do before they hand your details over to their customers.

For example *"Classic Rock & Pop covers"* and then a list covering some of the acts whose material you play. If you're an original act you need a statement of what you're about.

"Original guitar based trio whose influences include..."

You get the idea.

c) Contact details
Make sure no-one has any problems being able to get in touch and book your act. Get your phone numbers (mobile & home) and email address on the CD if that's the format you're using.

d) Venue Quote
Quotes or testimonials from satisfied customers are priceless as I well know from all my years in selling. In Step 13 I'll talk you through this in more detail but for now know that whenever you get a venue manager telling you how good your performance is, you should ask if you can quote him. Then, if his venue has some prestige, get that quote onto the CD or wherever the MP3 is accessed from. If his isn't a well-known venue use a number of positive quotes with the demo and name the venues.

"Best band we've had on all year" – George & Dragon, Ilfington
"Fantastic" – Reggie's Bar, Sortford

Generally when you ask people if you can quote them, they'll think you're joking but I've never found anyone who has a problem with it. To be honest, you can probably get away without asking them because you're not naming them in person.

What if you don't have any positive quotes you can use? What if you haven't gigged yet? Put a suitable positive statement on the CD in inverted commas, like you'd see on a DVD cover for example.

"All the Country classics in a memorable live show"

Finally, a word about MP3s versus CDs. Once you have your music demo produced and on your PC ready for transferring to CD, you can obviously offer it in either format to the venue. You could ask them when the topic of a demo comes up. Personally I prefer to stick with the CD whenever I can because of the number of jobs this one little package can do, i.e. points a-d above. If you're sending an MP3 you'll need a separate band picture, contact details and quotes etc. These need to be all together at the same time to get the whole of your message across. Separate items can't guarantee that. If your MP3s are being accessed via your website (if you have one), then you're relying on someone taking the time to click into it.

7.8 What more could they want?

Sometimes you may be asked for a "Band Bio". This basically means some further background info on the band. This is usually sent with the demo when it's asked for. The good news is that you should have done most of the work for this when you were looking at your strengths and uniqueness in the very first step.

You need to craft this into a couple of paragraphs that you can use to describe your band. Once this is done, you can use the same couple of paragraphs whenever you have to write to a venue after the initial phone conversation (this is quite common with hotels for example).

So, you understand how to create the powerful selling tool of a demo that stands out from the crowd. Now you need to approach the venues.

Step 8: **How to easily get gigs over the phone**

The system that you're going to use for getting gigs over the phone involves 2 stages.

Firstly, you make one phone call to find out who books the acts. Then a day or so later you phone up and specifically ask to speak to the person in question. The reason for doing it this way is so you can speak with some authority and sound like you know what you're doing on the 2nd phone call. It's not unusual for whoever answers the phone to screen their boss's phone calls, especially if they think you're trying to sell him/her something. So, if you sound confident that you know who you want on that 2nd call, they'll be far less likely to put you off and in most cases will put you straight through to the person you want.

8.1 **How to make yourself feel confident about the call**

Many people find it difficult to talk with confidence over the telephone. This can be especially true when you're trying to persuade someone to do something which is really important to you.

Keep in mind this: You've already done the hard part by learning how to play an instrument or how to sing. If you can do that, you'll be able to follow and succeed with this sequence.

The main point to remember here is the key to all successful selling. It's something we touched on early in Step 4:

Concentrate on what you can do for them – not what they can do for you.

Great, but what does this actually mean? Don't worry about whether they'll give you a booking. Keep your focus on how the uniqueness of your act (remember Step 1?) could encourage people to go to their venue and boost their takings.

Start with writing out your script for each of the 2 phone calls. Put this statement at the top of each page:

"Thank goodness I'm calling; this venue desperately needs my band".

Don't laugh this off as ridiculous just yet. You'll only need to glance at this as you make each phone call and you'll be reminded that you're there to **help** the venue and entertainment booker – not just take money from them for playing. This will automatically reduce any discomfort or stress you might feel from phoning.

8.2 <u>The simple call for information – the 1st call</u>

As mentioned earlier, the first stage is to find out the person who books the band. The script for this call is as follows:

Venue: *"Hello Fox and Herring how can I help you?"*

You: *"Oh hello there I wonder if you <u>could</u> (stress word) **help me. I'm just trying to find the name of the person responsible for booking the bands and entertainment?"***

Generally at this point they will give you the name you need. Check the spelling. They might ask if you want to be put through at this time but just say no, you're going to contact them later with some information. If they ask you why you want to know the name, or who you are, simply say you run a local band and would like their name so you can contact them at a later date to introduce yourself.

It's important not to give too much away to this person who isn't in a position to book you. The more info you give them (i.e. if you try to start selling yourself to them), the stronger the chance you'll be told they "have all the bands we need/aren't looking to take new bands on" etc. So keep it brief and businesslike.

There's another possible outcome for this initial call. When you ask for the name of the entertainment booker the voice on the other end might say: *"Me"*.

If this happens you'll need to go into selling mode straight away (see 2nd stage phone call beneath).

8.3 <u>Seeing how you can help them – the 2nd call</u>

Here's something not everyone is aware of. There are good and bad times of the week and day to call venues. It's similar to when you get a call centre phoning your home to try and sell you something. It never ceases to amaze me how some can phone me in the middle of the match on TV for example.

Anyway, the best days to call them, in my experience, are Monday, Tuesday or Wednesday. Forget Thursday, Friday or Saturday as they'll be too busy with customers and Sunday is generally not a day anyone wants to think about business.

As for timings, generally the best time is after the lunchtime trade (assuming they have some). So I schedule my calls from around 2.30pm on a Monday-Wednesday. What if you're unable through other commitments to hit these times? The next best is generally early evening after 6 and before the evening trade starts and the venue gets busy.

Here's what you say:

Venue: *"Hello Fox and Herring. How may I help you?"*

You: *"Oh hello. Is Dave Handistone* about today?"*

(* the name you were given yesterday)

At this point they'll either say yes and put you through or no and let you know when he will be in. If they say he is in, just before they put you through they might ask who it is calling. Just give them your name. Don't mention what the call is about (remember giving as little away as possible to the "gatekeeper"?). If they press you as to what the call's about just say:

You: *"it's in connection with the live bands/entertainment at the Fox & Herring".*

Generally the booker will be interested in taking your call from any of the above information. In both cases it's not immediately apparent that yours is a "sales" call. This means they will at least hear your first few words before deciding whether they're interested or not.

8.4 <u>Your vital first words to the booker</u>
Keep in mind before and during making this call what your objectives for the call are. Ideally, you'll take a booking with

this call. Second best would be for you to let them have a demo which they can listen to and make a decision on. At the very least, in the case of them having no interest at this time, you want an agreement to contact them again at a later date as things develop.

Venue booker: *"Hello, Dave Handistone?"*

You: *"Afternoon Dave. My name's Chris Adams from a band called Shakeshaft; do you have a quick second?"*

This exact approach is very important. It does 3 things:

a) Makes you sound friendly and non-threatening.
People can be nervous about what they feel is a sales call, something where they'll be called upon to make a decision. The last thing you want is to come across as being pushy.

b) Checks whether it's convenient to talk at that time.
Consider the contrast with call centre intrusions you might receive yourself where the caller ploughs on with his pitch without any apparent interest in whether you have time to listen.

c) Reassures them that this discussion will only take up a very short amount of their valuable time.
I don't know about you but I've often found myself in the middle of some sales person calling me where all I can think about is how quickly I can get this person off the phone. In the case of your call, you've already told them this should only take seconds.

Generally, when you've asked if they can spare a few seconds they will say *"Yes"*. If they say they can't because they're too busy, going out or whatever, ask them:

"When might be a better time to call?" Make a note of their answer and schedule a follow-up using your organiser (page 41).

8.5 <u>They're all ears: now what?</u>

You: *"I manage/play in a local* **(you might choose to name the place, for example, if they're in Luton, try** *"Luton-based")* **covers band."**

"We've got a considerable following & we play at places like...."

The mention of where you play is obviously only relevant once you have somewhere you can quote.
In the above statement to the venue you're trying to encourage them that:

a) You may bring a few people in to his establishment when you play ("considerable following")
b) You are of a reasonable standard to have played at the venues you mention
c) He may be missing out if he doesn't consider you.

What do you do though if you really have no track record of gig-playing to speak of? You're going to have to bluff it. Instead of naming venues simply say:

"We play at pubs and clubs in the south east" (for e.g.).

Move on quickly (i.e. without pause from the last statement) to:

You: *"I've just got one question really if I may"*

This again stresses you'll be brief but it will also:

a) Involve them in the conversation (they know a direct question is coming up and they'll be expected to answer – everyone likes to give their opinion on things)

b) They won't feel any of the pressure they might from a hard-selling phone call. You're <u>asking,</u> not <u>telling</u> them something.

You*: "Does your current supply of bands fully meet your needs or do you feel there may be some room for improvement?"*

This is a killer question. When you stop and think about it, doesn't the answer to this kind of question determine whether anyone ever buys anything?

What can the venue booker say to this?

There's the possibility he may be very happy with all the bands he has. If that's the case...

You: *Ok I understand. If it's OK with you I'll stay in touch as things develop, just in case circumstances do change at your end.*

He or she will readily agree to this. You simply schedule a further contact for yourself at some point in the future. A couple of months is usually about right. We'll consider how to covert this kind of "satisfied" venue in more detail when we come to look at keeping in touch with venues in Step 17.

The more immediately positive responses to the killer question will be:

Venue Booker: *"there's always room for improvement"* (if I had a £ for every time I've heard that said back to me in this situation….).

Alternatively, more often than you'd imagine you'll be told they are actively looking at sourcing new bands. Often, it seems, because agents are charging venues too much and a good band without an agent is nearly always less expensive.

8.6 <u>Closing the deal and the call</u>

In either of those cases there's a booking for the taking. Your next question should be:

You: *"How would we go about being considered for the Fox & Herring?"*

There are now only 3 things between you and the gig.

    a)   Is your material suitable?
    b)   Is your ability and act good enough for their venue?
    c)   How much do you charge?

This is the point, once you've asked the question high-lighted above, that these three potential obstacles to the gig will need to be aired. You yourself should get them out in the open to some degree, otherwise they'll be niggling him and he may decline any involvement without expressing his fears and giving you the chance to overcome them.

Let's look at each of them.

a) <u>Is your material suitable?</u>
The benefit of a wide variety of musical styles (within reason) becomes obvious here. If all you play is thrash metal and you've approached a pub that mainly features

Soul and Motown acts you're in trouble. You obviously haven't done your research from Step 4 properly.

When I'm asked about what sort of music we play I reel off a small string of artists (say, 7 or 8) from the 1960's through to the present day. Artists which cover a reasonably wide spectrum. That way, even if they don't generally feature bands like mine, they can see that we play some commercial material which their customers should at least have heard of. Assuming you've researched their usual kind of acts though, it's enough to just reassure them with:

"Classic country standards like most of your acts but with... (here comes some of the uniqueness you offer)...*a lot of audience involvement/additional contemporary numbers/set lists tailored in individual venues"* (delete as appropriate for you)

b) Is your act "good enough" for their venue?
Once you've got a couple of well-known venues on your band's CV it can often be enough just to mention these, telling the venue you're regulars at such and such etc. In these circumstances your "quality" becomes far less of an issue and is often not even questioned.

But what if you don't? This is where your demo comes in vital. You should offer to let him hear for himself so that he doesn't just have to take your word for it. You'll need to get it to him A.S.A.P. and then call him a few days later for his thoughts. Schedule this in your organiser.

c) How much do you charge?
Once you're asked this question by the venue you should be home and dry. Your immediate response though is this:

"It depends to some extent, on timings. Would you be looking at two sets? And what time would you want us to start and finish?"

This is vital information. Three sets, the third of which is expected to finish at 1.00 am is very different to 2 sets where you finish at 11pm. (Different not least of all because of how the band members will feel the next morning).

Once you have your answer, I suggest you quote a figure which is higher than the minimum you established in Step 3. If you decided £200 was your bare minimum, you might quote £250 for example. Remember, we're talking about price levels for an unestablished band here.

If they recoil at the asking price, ask them what their budget is. If it's acceptable to you, say you could do a "one-off" at that price and suggest if they're happy with you the fee could be looked at for future bookings. This way they will feel they have a bargain.

If their budget isn't acceptable, tell them:

"I couldn't get them out for that figure but we could probably do you a one off because (you're local to us/ the timings etc) for .... **(state your minimum).**

Pause at this point. Then ask:

"Presumably you'd want posters in advance?"

This will reassure them that you'll help with some advertising for the event (we'll cover this aspect more fully in the next Step).

If they can't meet your minimum price, you'll have to tell them you wouldn't possibly be able to play for the figure they have in mind. Thank them for their time and say you'll keep them posted on future developments with the band in case circumstances change. Basically, you'll keep in touch via your press releases and newsletter (Steps 9 and 17) for when their budget changes or they become more convinced of your value to them.

This *"How much do you charge?"* question will obviously have to be faced if the venue requires a demo. When you call them back for their opinion on what they listened to, then you'll proceed to this point (providing they're happy with what they heard of course!)

It's important that you remember these phone calls are part of a numbers game. The more you practise and the more venues you talk to, the more gigs you'll get.

It may take you 10 or more *"Thanks, but no thanks"* before you get a booking.

Believe me though, once you get your first taste of euphoria on converting a potential venue into a gig over the phone – you'll be hooked. You'll want more of the same. Just make sure you commit to making a set minimum number of phone calls to new venues per month and with practise you'll have all the work you can handle.

Later on we'll look at how we can keep in touch with all our potential venues and move even the most doubtful closer and closer to booking us with each passing week. For now, let's see what we can do in preparation for a successful gig night once one is booked.

How to easily get gigs over the phone

Step 9: **What else can you do for the venue?**

It won't surprise you to hear that once the gig is confirmed or you've had a "No" and understand their current situation re: bands, you're going to carry on setting your act apart from others.

How do you do this?

Firstly, let's look at when you've got the booking over the phone. How should you follow this up?

9.1 <u>Let people **INSIDE** the venue know</u>

You'll remember from the last step that once the gig was confirmed you reassured your contact by saying you assumed he would require posters. Unless he said he didn't want them you should arrange to get some to him by about 2 weeks before your gig, at the latest.

Any earlier than this and you risk the posters being lost as they're put away until closer to your appearance. Any later than a fortnight before and you'll miss letting his key weekend punters know there's a great live band coming up.

If it's possible, take the posters in person and meet the booker concerned. If he's not around, say hello to whatever bar staff there are. Introduce yourself and let them know you're playing there in a couple of weeks as you leave the posters for the manager/booker.

If you can't get there in person (and no other band member can), mail them out with a little note saying something like:

"Dear Dave, Please find posters as discussed for the gig on 27th April. Look forward to seeing you then."

What about the posters themselves? What should be on them?

Here are some key considerations for you when you design your own:

a) Leave an empty box in the centre of the poster so the venue themselves can put in the date of your appearance. This way you won't have to alter the poster each time you mail or hand them out to a different venue.

The next info for the posters ties in with what you put on the demo and you can save yourself time and effort by using exactly the same:

b) **Picture of the band on the posters**. Personally I prefer to go for black and white for the photograph as this is cheaper to print in quantity.

c) **Give the punters a clue for what to expect by listing the artists whose music you play**. You don't need them all, but like on the demo try to show as wide a range as possible. If you're an original band, briefly describe your music/genre/influences on the poster.

d) **Include a quote (or two) from satisfied venues**. As with the demo, if you don't yet have anyone to quote you can still put something in *"inverted commas"*. Just like I did then.

e) **Use some colour on the poster – to catch the eye.** Possibly the band name (which should be at the top of the page), the phrase "live music" (so the reader can see in an instant what the poster is all about) and the logo/name of the venue which you're quoting in "d" above. Include your website address or Myspace page too if you have them.

How many do you send or give out each time and what size? If you're doing them on your own PC and this can handle A3 (large size) as well as A4, then give them 2 of each. Failing that 4 x A4 will work fine.

You can design your poster in something like MS Publisher and either get them printed in quantity by a local printer or (as I prefer to do) knock them out on my own colour printer as needed.

9.2 <u>Letting people OUTSIDE the venue know</u>

You'll need to check with the venue that they're happy for press publicity for the gig, but if so, exposure can often be simpler to achieve than you'd imagine.

Assuming you're comfortable with being in the local papers, you need to establish:

a) **Does the venue currently advertise in the press at all?** If so, this will be the place to target with a press release for your forthcoming appearance.

b) **Contacts for the relevant papers (whether the venue advertises in them or not).** For example, you should target the paper which is local to where the venue is. Also your own home town paper (if this is different from the venues') along with those papers in other band member's home towns. Find the publication's phone number from inside the paper and ask for the name & email address of the person responsible for "Entertainment" features. If it doesn't have one, ask for the "News Editor".

c) **Deadline days for news stories**. Whether the local paper is a daily or a weekly, you'll need to know which day of the week they need your press release so you can hit the edition most relevant to your forthcoming gig. Just call your contact at the paper (news or entertainment editor) once you've established them, and ask what their "copy deadlines" are. (No need to tell them anything about your "news story" at this point.

9.3 Getting the local press interested in you

Take a look through your local rag and you'll be amazed at some of the "news" they seem interested in. Someone's new allotment, a zebra crossing that needs a coat of paint or a playgroup outing to the zoo. There's really no reason they shouldn't be interested in a local group of musicians playing at a local venue.

The trick is to find some form of "angle", something a little unusual about your act or the fact you're playing at the venue in question. You can refer to the qualities you established about your band back in Step 1 for some inspiration here.

Here's an example of a headline I used for a press release submitted to a local paper (via email) about my band:

"We're coming home"

Interesting headlines are vital to any news story so if you can think of something eye-catching and do the thinking for the newspaper (rather than them have to create a headline), so much the better. This headline was shamelessly ripped off the England football song/lament (topical at the time – during the last World Cup) and referred to my band playing a gig close to my home rather than those we usually played a little further a field.

In the email I mentioned the following:

- Where we usually played (i.e. the out of town venues)
- The fact that this local appearance was a "special event" (because we didn't normally play that locally)
- A couple of the unique qualities of the band (see Step 1).

I went on to give details of the forthcoming local gig (start time, phone number) and also added my own contact details and a jpeg of the band in action.

The last 2 points are crucial. If they like the sound of the "story" they may well call you up for additional details. A good picture can, on its own, make all the difference between a dull-sounding piece of news and something that really catches the eye – so make sure you attach a jpeg to every news story you send out. (We'll look at building up a good library of the best kind of pictures in Step 12).

Now you've seen what else you can do for the venue over and above just turning up and playing once the gig is booked. In the next section, Part Three, we'll look at the components of a successful gig night, everything from what to wear, right through to how to book further gigs as soon as you come off stage.

What else can you do for the venue?

PART THREE: **Gig Night**

10.   Creating a memorable live show every time

11.   Advertising while you play

12.   Take photos

13.   Use what people say

14.   How to make sure you get paid & more
      bookings

<u>Step 10</u>: **Creating a memorable live show every time**

Before you start your show there are 3 things you can and should do in preparation.

10.1 <u>Dress up or dress down?</u>

In reality you won't have to change your look much from venue to venue and if you intend playing all the same type of venues then you probably won't need to change at all.

However, if you plan to cover hotels, pubs, clubs, weddings & private parties etc. then there may be a little adjustment needed. If you like feeling relaxed in jeans and t-shirt for pubs then, as we saw in Step 2, you can have slightly smarter versions and newer, more conservative t-shirts for slighter smarter venues. That's what my band does anyway. If you want to "move up" towards wearing a collar but don't want anything too fancy then a polo shirt, short sleeved and cotton, is a good bet.

The key is to be comfortable while you play but not look as if you've come straight from working on the market stall to play at someone's party. Just give each gig a little thought before hand and try to visit the venue when another band's playing if that's at all possible.

10.2 <u>Let the "hirer" have some input into what you play</u>

This is especially important for private functions or indeed anywhere the audience might be more mixed or not your band's "usual" type of crowd.

Once your name gets around, if people enjoy watching your act, you WILL get approached to play at private functions. At weddings, for example, you should offer to have a meeting with the bride and groom well in advance of the function, to discuss the material. Of course you won't fill your sets with their specific requests, but you'll get a great reputation if you can at least respond to some of their particular favourites (and leave anything out that might offend Grandma in the audience.)

As part of your pitch to any new venue, when they ask about the material you play, you should be giving them as wide a list as possible but then adding:

"Of course we can tailor the material if you have any special requirements".

9 out of 10 of them never do. But I know it increases a band's opportunities just offering that service. It takes away possible reasons for not hiring you.

On the subject of private functions, if you want to offer the complete service you might be able to offer a "D.J." facility as well if required. You can then claim any D.J. fee as part of your agreed payment for the night.

If you have a lap top or MP3 player you can load them with material chosen by the person who booked you, and hook them up to the PA. Aside from any special announcements that may be required (1st dance for the bride and groom /cake for the birthday boy etc). You don't need to get involved in all the usual inane D.J. chatter while the music is playing. In fact it's better if you don't. You simply let the music player do its work. The benefit of no D.J. chat here is that the band very obviously becomes the highlight/focal point of the evening – rather than a little interruption to the "real event" which is the D.J. nonsense. This is the exact approach that works for us.

10.3 <u>Rent-a-crowd</u>

The final thing you can do in advance of gig night (particularly if you know the venue is struggling for numbers) is to invite fans/friends/family to the gig. You could even take one or two of them along if they have no transport and you have space in your car or van. Even the girlfriends/boyfriends of the band members can swell the numbers of a small crowd. Then as you progress people will ask when and where you're playing next.

If you keep these people on some kind of database (or even a simple list) you can text or email them to alert them to a future gig in their area. The alternative to this of course is to have a website which lists down forthcoming gigs. You can then direct any enquiries to your site.

You may not be surprised to learn that I'm not a great fan of listing your gigs on your website. Personally I don't want another band using my website as a directory of venues to call and consequently introducing new competition for us. (You remember Step 4 earlier - "Where do you find venues?"). The way round this is to invite visitors to your website to subscribe to gig updates.

Using this method you have some control over who sees what information relating to your band.

You might like to check out the automated service called Aweber (www.aweber.com) that we use. Basically, at the start of every month we email subscribers ("fans") with details of where we're playing over the next 4 weeks. We can also send reminders of upcoming gigs in between times if we need to try and swell numbers at a particular gig for whatever reason.

So, gig-night is finally here. What are the things you can do to set you apart from the usual run-of-the-mill band or act?

10.4 <u>Your set list(s)</u>

The key facts to remember about your sets are:

a) *Make an immediate impact.*
This involves more than just a number you play well. You shouldn't start with a slow number, even in the first set. Kick off with something to wake everyone up. You can always slow things down again with the second number, but at least you'll be giving them a taster of what's to come. At the very least a reason to hang around for the second set when traditionally a band's material livens up.

Not only should the first number of your first set be one of your strongest ones. It should also be well-known but just as importantly, showcase as many of your performing qualities as possible. For example, not all our numbers have backing vocals and/or a lead break. The numbers which start each of our sets always do though. Make sure your first numbers showcase as many of your strengths as a performer/ performers as possible. In our case, we start with the first number we used on our demo (see step 7).

b) *End strongly.*
Your ending doesn't need to display everything but the kitchen sink here (like you may have done when the set started), but you want something which ideally ends with a bang (suddenly). It should also be an up-tempo number which people generally respond well to. Obviously, if

you're new to gigging, only time will tell what people will respond to so you'll have to use some guess work at first.

Basically, to summarise points a) and b) above; as one gig-weary guitarist once said to me:

"Do your best number first, 2nd best last...and in the middle all the s***".

A little extreme but you get the idea.

c) *The second set should be more up-tempo.*
You might like to think of it as your "party" set. People will usually have had a few drinks by the second set so are normally up for a good time. Your job is to give it to them. Start off strongly again and ideally group songs from similar eras together (assuming you're playing covers).

In time you'll get to know quickly which set any new song should go into.

d) *Sets should each be around 10 songs long.*
This is generally true but, depending on how long you've agreed to play, you may find you need a couple of extra numbers for the second set. You should also save something memorable which usually goes down well as your encore.

If you're struggling for enough material when you're starting, you can always claim to have been asked by a member of the audience to play something you've already done as your encore. Just make sure it's one that went down well!

10.5 <u>Dealing with audience requests</u>

As you get more experienced and build up your repertoire of songs, the time will come when you're able to respond to an audience crying out for any particular artist's material – by actually doing one. Until then, it's useful to make a note of anything you're asked for more than once and if you like the material in question – learn some for future gigs. Generally, what's popular in more than once place will be useful feedback. This is the easy way to choose which new songs to add to your material.

If you're asked for something during a performance that you can't do, simply tell them that you don't do anything at the moment but that you'll try learning something for next time.

10.6 <u>Getting the audience involved</u>

Unless part of your "unique attraction" is to appear unsociable and make your audience angry, it's a good idea to try and get them involved in the show.

Think about your material. Rather than just announcing what each of the songs are, you can ask a question relevant to the song title. For example, say you're playing *White Wedding* by Billy Idol. You can ask:

"Any newlyweds here tonight?"

If you get a response, tell them you're playing this song for them. If not ask something like:

"Anyone thinking of getting married... newly divorced.... thinking of getting divorced but not told their partner?" etc.

Then dedicate the song to them. Just get a little creative with some of your songs and see what you can do. A word of warning, don't do this with every song as you'll drive people crazy.

You don't want to recite chapters of *War and Peace* in between numbers, but at least talk to your audience, even if it's only to thank them for their applause. All of this will help you break down the psychological barriers that can exist between an act and their audience.

Another way to get your audience involved is to establish eye contact with different people as you're playing and smile if the moment calls for it. Too many acts are more concerned with looking cool. It might look great but it doesn't necessarily encourage your audience to relax and have a good time. So, scan the room when you're playing for anyone who seems into it, let them know you've seen them and appreciate it. A simple look and a smile can do this.

10.7 <u>What to do if "disaster" strikes</u>

Finally a quick word about how to prevent an accident at the gig turning into a disaster. One night while playing our lead singer/guitarist broke a string, twice. Because he was the front man who did most of the audience chat, there were long pregnant pauses while he replaced his string and tuned up. This taught us that we had to plan in advance for most eventualities. Just in case we have a similar experience again we have one number I can sing and which doesn't require his guitar to be played on it on standby. Similarly, if I have a problem with my bass we have an acoustic "unplugged" number we can quickly slip into. If the drummer uncontrollably needs to visit the gent's mid-set, (don't laugh, I've seen this happen), we have something we can play for a few minutes while he's gone.

It might be a good idea to think of what could help you if you have temporary problems on gig night. The idea is to keep the whole show running smoothly and so ensure a good reaction, hopefully.

So, you now have some tips for making the gig one to remember (for all the right reasons) for the audience. This is enough to get you started. If you feel that you need more details on this aspect, you could always check out www.gig-getter.com/rousethecrowdebook.htm

Now let's see some simple ideas on how you too can be sure to benefit most from every performance.

Step 11: **Advertising while you play**

We've looked at posters and advertising before the night of the gig. These can go some way towards giving contact details to interested parties while you're onstage. However, I suggest you go further than this.

11.1 Get your name in front of the whole audience

I've lost count of the number of bands and other acts I've watched who get up on stage and anyone wandering in to watch them would have no idea who they are.

Many acts don't have any mention of their name on the stage while they're up there let alone a contact number. If you're going to maximise the gigs you play, you'll want to make sure that, if people like what they see and hear it's easy for them to do something about it while it's still at the front of their minds.

We get a great deal of further work as a result of playing gigs. People see us and want us for their own private functions. This is where all our lucrative wedding and party work has come from. Some people though, can feel awkward about approaching a band to ask whether they could hire them. If you advertise the fact you're for hire, you invite them to approach you. Some won't approach you on the night probably because they're too shy or intimidated. However, if you get the name of your act there so everyone can see it while you're playing and at least one contact phone number (or website details) people can make a note and contact you when it suits them.

11.2 <u>Make your name known</u>

You could put your name on a backdrop behind you (like Paul Weller's Jam did when they were starting out if you're old enough to remember them). However, including a phone number there would probably look a little too crass and might not be easily seen. Far better to get something more subtle. We had stickers made up and use them on the back of the stage monitors. That way, they're clear and readable to all concerned but are not so in your face that they detract from the show.

They're much more efficient and cost effective than the business cards we used to take to the shows and give out if they were asked for. Even if people have no intention of hiring a band themselves they may mention your name (because they'll see it on stage) to interested parties even if they're only passing through the venue for a quick drink.

If you don't advertise while you play you're wasting an important opportunity to sell your act to people. This can and should be another important tool in your gig-getting efforts. Don't be like most other acts and neglect it. There's really nothing to it and it will work well for you.

Now let's take a look at another key aspect of making gig night work for you - photography.

Step 12: **Take photos**

Another often neglected opportunity to help you promote your band is with photos. Get a friend or family member to take pictures – particularly on gig night.

Pictures of you rehearsing or portrait pictures are fine and can have their uses but you should be aiming to build up a good catalogue of snaps from every gig you play.

These can be used for posters, if you want to freshen up your original design, press releases (see Step 9) as well as your newsletters.

A couple of important points here that are not immediately obvious:

12.1 **Don't forget your audience**
You'll find it very useful to get pictures of more than just the band members in action. You want to show people enjoying themselves while you're playing. This can be a good motivator when other venues are thinking about booking you.

There are a few ways you can get pictures of the audience:

a) *Use your own phone/camera while on stage between numbers.*
You'll have to do this sparingly or it can look slightly ridiculous. However, the audience will often enjoy the involvement and may pose in an exaggerated fashion, which can be useful. There is a draw-back here though, obviously you can't take pictures while you're playing so that's likely

81

to mean the band (and so audience too), won't be in "full flow" while you snap.

b) <u>*Get a friend to come onto the stage with you and take photos from there.*</u>
This will work better than a) in terms of you having no playing restrictions but it can look a little over the top to the audience.

c) <u>*Get a friend to wander behind the bulk of the audience.*</u>
My favourite because it looks less "contrived". In fact it can appear as if the photographer is just an enthusiastic audience member compelled to start taking pictures. The benefit in terms of the pictures taken will be that they include both the audience AND the band.

Experiment with each of these options and see which suits you best.

12.2. <u>Include ALL the band</u>
As you build up your portfolio of snaps with each gig, make sure you have decent ones of all the band members. You'll need these when you use them for publicity. It can also be disheartening for any particular band member if he or she continually only gets a minor spot in photographs. This can be especially true for drummers who tend to be easily hidden behind their kits. Keep tabs on the pictures you have in your collection and brief the photographer to concentrate on the missing elements as well as adding to the usual suspects like the lead singer & audience.

12.3 <u>Don't let your wardrobe let you down</u>
Even if your "look" is jeans and a t-shirt, just make sure you rotate what you're wearing from gig to gig a little to get some variation and interest into the pictures. The danger, if

you don't, is that it can look as if all the pictures are of the same gig. You want to let people know you are playing regularly (even if to start with "regularly" is not very often).

12.4 <u>Use venue "landmarks"</u>

If the venue has a logo on the wall or something that is known (the metallic logo on the wall behind the stage at the Hard Rock Cafe, or the "Cigar Smoker" on the wall at the old Cuban Nights), try to include these in some pictures of gig night. These will add authenticity and credibility to your publicity efforts.

That's enough about using what people can **see** from gig night. What about what's **said** on the night?

Take photos

Step 13: **Use what people say**

Working in sales for as long as I have, I've learnt the value of getting "3rd party endorsements" on my claims for whatever I'm selling.

With the band and gig-getting situation this translates as:

Collecting positive things people say about you and repeating these to other people to help you get more gigs.

We looked at this a little in Step 7 where I suggested you put a positive quote with your demo. This step, though, is all about making sure you don't miss any opportunity with anything positive the venue might say about your band on gig-night itself.

13.1 **The power of praise**
Keep your ears open for anyone managing or involved with any venue saying something good about your band. Then thank the person for their praise and, smiling, ask them whether you can quote them.

9 out of 10 people will be more than happy for their words to be quoted though most will think you're just being funny and you have no intention of using them.

13.2 **What do you do with the quotation?**
Once again the answer is simple. You use the positive statements on your advertising. ("Advertising" being your posters and your demos). These quotes will work to influence the reader in the same way reviewer quotes work on DVD cases or underneath product details at Amazon for example.

There are 2 approaches to using quotes or testimonials. One is what I call the "volume" approach, where you list down a string of all the positive statements you have from whatever source. The other is the "more is less" route. Using fewer is my favourite approach but to make it work you'll really need a statement from a well-known venue. Our band now uses a simple, single one-liner on all our posters and our demo.

If you don't have anything as immediately recognisable as a big name venue (and most of us don't when we're first starting out), you probably ought to opt for the longer list approach. Here, the fact that many of these venues may be small bars and pubs will be reduced greatly because so many people are saying good things about you.

Obviously you can only work with what you have and so when you're just starting out you'll have only a few, if any, quotes to use. However, you can make sure this list grows as fast as your gigs. When you collect your money after every performance, ask the venue booker or manager:

"Was that ok for you?"

No matter if the venue has had better, this question invites a positive statement. You'll find that most come up with some form of response which you can edit for your future use.

13.3 **How to use quotations to sell your band**

We saw how to lay your quotes out when we looked at how to use them on your demo CD. Basically like this:

"Worth Every penny" – Dog and Herring, Ipswich

"Fantastic!" - Fullchester Royal Legion

The important point is that on gig-night you never stop asking and listening for positive statements about your band. You won't have to use them all. You can obviously cherry-pick and replace old ones with great new ones as you go on. Just make sure you never stop collecting them!

All that remains now on gig night is to get paid and try to agree further bookings.

Use what people say

<u>Step 14</u>: **How to make sure you get paid & more bookings**

Along with putting on a memorable show for people to enjoy, encouraging members of the audience who might want to book you (through your onstage adverts), collecting pictures and quotes, you need to make sure:

a)   You get paid for the night
b)   You get at least one follow-up gig.

14.1 <u>Show me the money</u>
This is often straightforward, in that the person who booked you (or their representative) will come over to you after the show with the money. There will be times though when this doesn't seem to be happening and so you need to know how to ask in the best possible way.

If you're collecting testimonials/quotes as I advised in the last step, you'll be offering them an opportunity to sort your money out when you ask them: *"Was that ok for you?"*

Some will either pay you at that point (as well as hopefully giving a decent quote), or make some reference to getting the money ready for you later when you've finished packing up.

You may feel awkward asking for money and so if there's no mention of it when you go about collecting your testimonial, approach them again when you've nearly finished packing up and are almost ready to leave.

"Ok, we're about ready to go now".

This is usually all you need to provoke the money and you haven't even mentioned it. If this still does not get a response, you're going to have to ask outright. Just follow your last statement to them up with:

"We just need to sort the money out now".

That will do it.

14.2 <u>Strike while the iron's still red-hot</u>

I always give the opportunity for the venue to book us again on gig-night rather than wait until the following week and call them. The reason for this is that if you've gone down well they'll be at their most enthusiastic on gig-night itself rather than the following week when it's become a memory.

So, when you've popped the question about the money and they've paid you, simply ask:

"Do you want to sort out another date now or shall I call you next week?"

This is deceptively simple. It's based on a sales technique which assumes they are going to do what you want them to (i.e. book you again) and it offers them 2 alternatives; booking you now or next week. Now, the reality is they may not fancy you again for their venue. If that's the case they'll probably tell you to call them next week and then when you do they won't take your call.

However, don't assume that if you are asked to call the following week it means they don't want you back. Many venue bookers don't organise themselves enough to have their bookings diary with them on the night. You should always make sure you do, though. Always be ready, willing and able to take a booking. If they don't have their diary, try to find out a convenient day and time the following week to call them back and stick to it.

If they do have their diary and seem keen to book it, agree the date in question and then push further. Assuming the next one is for a month's time, let's say March for example, ask:

"We are being asked about April too already, do you want to put one in for then as well now?"

They can only say no and you will have again stressed how busy/popular your act is by indicating how people are trying to book you some way in advance. It may be that they don't want you on every month – or every four weeks is too often for your own liking. In this case you can suggest something a couple of months from the follow-up gig you've just agreed.

I've booked five additional gigs at a time using this method and the beauty with making these follow up dates on the night is:

a)   There's no phone call cost involved
b)   You can use the time you would have spent phoning them back on calling a new potential venue

So that's gig-night and really making it work for you. In the final section I'll be showing you how to accelerate your gig-getting efforts. We'll look at the importance of ongoing work, more about getting into the press and how to keep in touch with potential venues until they too are ready to book you.

PART FOUR: **Onwards and upwards**

15.   The easy way to fill your gig diary

16.   More ways you can use the press

17.   How to get venues to CALL YOU

Step 15: **The easy way to fill your gig diary**

We touched on this idea in the step we just looked at when I gave you some ideas for booking further gigs at the venue on gig-night. Now I want to spell out the importance of this.

15.1 <u>Repeat work at the same venue</u>

If you think about it, there's a cost to booking a gig at any new venue. This cost may only be the phone call you make to persuade them to book you and for your time taken to do this. It may, though, include the cost of producing, mailing or hand-delivering CDs, any number of phone calls to follow-up what they thought of the demo and then to make the booking.

However, when you've played somewhere before, and they give you further bookings on the strength of this, there are no further, what I call "marketing" costs. The more regular work like that you can establish, the less stress or worry you'll have about making further bookings.

Taking this to the extreme, if you can fill your diary with regular work, you'll never need to make another booking in the other ways I'm recommending.

Personally, I like a mix of both regular and new work. It keeps us fresh and on our toes. It exposes us to new audiences and with that, additional potential for private party and function work. I'd suggest your goal should be to establish a "backbone" of regular gigs which you play every few months or so and additional new venues/one-offs (which may or may not lead to additional regular work) on top of this.

Keep in mind that if private functions and parties are one of your goals and you're not getting all the work you want in that area, you'll need to either:

- – Improve your playing/mix of material
- – Improve your advertising of & at gigs
- – Expose yourself to more/new audiences

Now you know why you should be aiming to establish a line of regular venues I want you to consider one very effective and free way of getting your name around, using the press.

Step 16: **More ways you can use the press**

You know, from earlier in this manual, how to use the press to publicise a forthcoming appearance at a specific venue in order to attract more people to the gig. You should really be able to get all the work you need through the approaches I've detailed in Parts 1 and 2 of this manual, so any additional press exposure is really only for those who want to put themselves "out there" and maximise the number of people who know about them.

This approach can also be useful to help drive up your gig fees over time. As people see you in the press they will begin to convince themselves that you are somehow worthy of a larger fee than they might have otherwise believed.

Some band members may not be comfortable with their friends and neighbours seeing them mentioned in the local paper, so make sure you ok this kind of activity with all your band mates first.

So, if you're all keen on maximising your exposure through the press what can you do?

16.1 Establish your target publications

When we talked about press exposure to support a particular gig, we focussed on the paper local to that venue. When you're looking for an ongoing press presence you widen your target. Here you should include:

- Publications local to each of the band members

- Publications connected with any of the band member's pasts (where they were born/educated/worked etc)
- The trade press connected to any band members (say your drummer works in IT, target any IT trade magazines for example)
- Any specialised publications connected with band members (your bassist is a keen angler – target angling magazines)
- The music press

You may be wondering why the angling magazine for example, would be interested in anything to do with your band. You need to establish that connection. Your press release will centre on your bassist in the example above. You'll include jpegs of him on the riverbank (or wherever he casts his rod if you'll pardon the expression) and another with him in full flight (or as close as bassists get), on stage. Specialist magazines have to fill their pages with items of interest to their readers. In this example, many of the angling magazine readers will be interested to read a well constructed piece on "one of them" who also stars on stage in a successful act.

The trick here, with any of the categories of publications listed above, is to scan the pages of recent editions for ideas on how you construct your own "stories/releases".

16.2 <u>Send out regular press releases</u>

Once you have your target publications you should make it your goal to send them a release/story on a regular basis. How regular is this? It depends on 2 things:

- How often they publish a new edition
- How much of interest you have to say

If the publication is weekly you'll be pushing your imagination and probably their patience if you try to hit them every week with a new release. If they're monthly though this will be very possible.

Don't worry about getting on their nerves by frequently sending out releases to them. All publications live and die by their content and you're sending them "free" content which you have aimed and written precisely to be of interest to their readers.

16.3 <u>What do the press want to know?</u>
This is where you need to get creative. You need to be constantly on the look-out for newsworthy paragraphs you can send to them.

What makes a press release newsworthy?

You'll have established plenty of material when you examined what makes your band different back in Step 1. I don't know your own particular circumstances but examples (depending on the type of publication chosen) might include:

- Family man/Grandfather who has a double life as "secret" band member (you have an ageing lead guitarist)
- College student of particular area (who learns his musical skills at the college/showed no sign of any musical ability at said college – delete as appropriate) now performing across the area as part-time lead singer.

In our examples of publications from 16.1, if your drummer in IT gets a promotion, switches companies, completes a big project etc, hit the publication again and make sure they know.

A headline for the IT magazine might be:

"Drumming up a new direction"
(You go on to write a short paragraph about the new position the drumming IT guru is about to take, making sure you name your band and at least one of your unique qualities in the release).

Any angling awards or contests your bassist enters or wins for example should of course be fired at the angling magazine, again with your band name mentioned.

You should be continually looking for any opportunity to link your band with the relevant publication and gain a mention no matter how brief.

As far as the music press is concerned, even as a covers band there are opportunities to get your name in print.

Look for the free gig guide section and simply notify them with the details when and where you're playing each gig.

The key with all of these publications and what you can gain exposure for is, as I've stressed above, to monitor their pages for the kinds of things they're already covering. Do this, and then give them more of the same.

Whatever you send them, make sure you attach at least one good quality and relevant jpeg. It will massively increase your chances of publication.

Finally, a word about following up your press releases. Should you call each time and find out whether they have received the information, what they thought of it and whether they intend to publish it?

You can if you have nothing else to do. I've never bothered. I buy or try to look at the publication, if I remember, and it's always a big thrill to see your work has been used. But sensibly you'll have plenty of other things to do rather than chase your press releases. Just keep sending them out and checking the magazines concerned when you can. At the same time monitor the types of features and news they contain to help with your future releases, and then you'll have enough time to do things like work for a living, sleep or study.

Ok, we've done the press bit to death; let's have a closer look at making sure you stay in touch with all your prospective venues so that THEY call YOU.

More ways you can use the press

Step 17: **How to get venues to CALL YOU**

If you think about it, your initial phone call to a venue will only work if they have a "problem" with their acts or are open to trying to find new acts at that time. If they're satisfied with everything they have, you'll be very unlikely to succeed when you call.

Often you'll be told your details will be kept on file for when "circumstances change" and this can indeed happen. However, what you want is to keep your act fresh in their minds and make certain that when they do start looking for new bands, yours is the one that springs to mind first.

How do you do this? Well, short of phoning them on a regular basis and asking: *"So **now** do you need our act?"*, the best solution is simply to keep them informed about what your band is up to. The ideal way to do this is to publish your own newsletter.

Fear not, this doesn't have to be as grand as it sounds. You're looking for a simple one pager (A4) which you'll send out to all your prospective venues (and current regular ones if you see fit) a few times a year. Personally I prefer quarterly.

17.1 <u>Stay in touch</u>

What is the real purpose of the newsletter? The answer is simple:

- To encourage the venue that they need to book you.

Your newsletter should be a "brag sheet" which shows how well you're doing and gives reasons why you deserve to be booked. It can also be used to give the impression that the venue is missing out by not booking you.

Here are examples of some of the pieces I've included in newsletters for my band:

- Features on venues we're about to play at *(include items of interest about the place itself)#*
- Picture(s) from recent gigs *(try to get some of the audience enjoying themselves in the pic as well – or one of your unique features as established in Step 1 – in action)*
- List of recent gigs *(reassures venues you are in demand)**
- List of forthcoming gigs *(as above)**
- New equipment purchased *(reassures venue you are investing in your sound & band)*
- Mention of new numbers added to repertoire
- Availability of dates for them to book you *(make sure it seems "limited")*
- Contact details *(so they can call and book you)*
- A list of some of the artists you cover/your genre *(you can include this as a header in small italics across the top of the page)*
- Positive quotes about your act *(see Step 13)*

You can find out facts about most venues from their websites or if all else fails call the venue, tell them you're writing a piece about the gig for the local paper and ask them for some history of the venue.
* NB there is less to fear here about other people knowing details of the other places you play. The benefit with publishing your gig schedule via newsletters as opposed to

a website is that it goes to venues – not to other bands and to a large degree YOU control who sees this information.

17.2 **Create your newsletter**

You can make life easy for yourself if you use one of the numerous templates you'll find in Microsoft Publisher. Take one which catches your eye and adapt it as follows:

- Use only one side of one page of A4
- Call the newsletter by the name of your band/act
- Highlight your act name in colour or using your logo if you have one
- Add the word "News" alongside your name
- Limit the stories or features on the page to 4 or 5
- Include 3 or 4 small full-colour pictures on your newsletter

If you're struggling with how to write your newsletter, search in Google for "newsletter" and study how other "businesses" approach it. You can do worse than check out the way any good website approaches their "news" sections for ideas. On page 107 I've added an outline of the basic layout we use together with some simple ideas for stories.

On the subject of websites, what about using them to stay in touch with potential venues? If you can get an email address, or the venue has their own website, you might choose to send your newsletter electronically. Also, you might prefer to direct potential venues to your website. This latter approach is fine but it does seem to depend on one of 2 things to succeed:

a) The venue contact taking the trouble to get online and look at your site.

b) The venue contact being online in the first place so he /she can check out your details.

Personally I prefer the snail mail approach. That way I believe a venue manager can look at my newsletter while he's watching TV or whenever it suits him rather than having to be online. Also, in my experience, many of the smaller venues in particular still respond best to offline marketing.

Either way, you choose what you feel will work best for you. But stick to the pointers I've mentioned above.

17.3 <u>Following up</u>

Following–up a newsletter gives you a credible reason to get back in touch with the venue. I like to make a quick phone call just to check the venue has received the newsletter. At the very worst they'll thank you for it, you'll be in their minds again and they'll be even more likely to call you when they do have a need.

At best, they will make a booking on the strength of you calling to follow up. Just last month a new manager I'd never spoken to from a venue I was targeting called me after receiving our newsletter and gave me two bookings over the phone. This approach does work.

"Your Band"
(name & colour logo)

NEWS

Date

Venue's colour logo	Upcoming Gig at <u>name venue</u> (Story 1)	Story 3 New equipment added.

Story 3

New equipment added.

Details of additional musical kit purchased. Search manufacturer website for interesting/ impressive info on the equipment.

Story 1 column 1

Check venue web site for information and ideas. Have any "name" acts played here? How often do they have shows? If a hotel (for eg), has anyone well known stayed there?

Story 1 column 2

Story 1 column 3

-Entry cost (especially if 'FREE') and approx. show start time.

-Venue address and contact details (Some other venue owners may want to check you out in person.)

Picture of band member

Include footnote beneath naming him/ her.

News of recent gig
(Story 2)

Story 4

Details/ history of new numbers added to the set list.

Picture of band in action at the gig.

Ideally showing the audience having a good time.

Story 2 column 1

What happened? Was it a full house? Did you get an encore? Did you get asked back or further work else- where as a result?

Story 2 column 2

For more information on "Your Band" or to book the band, please call KEITH on 0161-800-000 or 07790-310604. (email: keithy@yahoo.co.uk)

A final word from me to you

I want to leave you with a word of encouragement. Taking charge of your gig-diary and avoiding leaving things to fate or the hope you might attract an agent, means talking to people about your band. Like any selling or promoting, all this is only a numbers game. The more people you talk to about your band, and the more people you approach to ask for the gig, the more gigs you'll get. It's that simple.

A persistent attitude in following the step by step principles laid out in "GIG-GETTER" will set you on your way. Come back to this manual on a regular basis as you begin to attract all the gigs you can handle. This will ensure you keep the advice in mind until it's "yours" without you even having to think about it. This will work in much the same way as you now know how to play your instrument or sing your song words. Remember how much there was to keep in mind when you first started learning? Remember trying to master that particular riff or song and thinking you'd never get it?

I wrote GIG-GETTER; HOW TO GET MORE GIGS THAN YOU CAN PLAY out of a real desire to help people let their musical and performing ability lead them to greater recognition, happiness and satisfaction than they dreamed possible. I wanted to write the most straightforward and specific manual available on the subject. In writing this I have withheld nothing as my "special secret". I've shared everything I use to get gigs.

Naturally I'd be delighted to hear from you.

Please feel free to share your success stories with me via *gareth@gig-getter.com*. Tell me which sections of the manual were particularly helpful, and give feedback on how you put these ideas into action. Also feel free to offer your suggestions for improvement. Let me know what still puzzles you.

The principles you've read here are tried, trusted and proven over and over. They work for those who use them. I extend a word of warning though. Take care if you do diligently follow the steps laid out in this manual, you could find yourself without enough nights in the month to satisfy all the venues who want you – just as I did. Good luck.

Sincerely, I take enormous pleasure in your achievements so please don't be shy about letting me know how good life becomes for you as a working performer, will you?

Gareth Bird

GIG-GETTER TIMETABLE

In "GIG-GETTER; HOW TO GET MORE GIGS THAN YOU CAN PLAY" I've tried to stress that, for your gig-getting venture to have the greatest chance of succeeding, you must plan and execute your steps carefully and consistently. This timetable will serve as your checklist to help you use your time wisely and carry out the actions in the most effective order. Bear in mind you may not fully understand some of the steps in this timetable until you've read right through the previous steps. When you need more specific details on any point in the timetable you should refer to the appropriate Step.

1.   Do BEFORE you start actively promoting your band

1.1   Work out what's different about your band. Study other local bands so you can get your uniqueness into clearer focus. If you don't feel you stack up well enough, make plans to change and improve.

1.2   Make sure you're good enough. Rehearse until you know your material inside out and get as much experience in front of audiences as is possible.

1.3   Gain agreement from all band members on exactly how often you want to play and for how much.

1.4   Establish a comprehensive list of places in your area where bands currently play.

1.5   Sign-up for additional free monthly gig-getting tips via **www.gig-getter.com**

2. Do when you start making initial contact over the phone

2.1 Create a gig diary for the band and distribute to all members.

2.2 Plan and produce your 5 minute demo.

2.3 Write and stick to a telephone script when calling venues.

2.4 Design a band poster that can be used in your venues.

3. Do when your promoting efforts start producing gigs

3.1 Use your findings from point 1.1 above to write an initial press release for the band.

4. Do every gig night

4.1 Make sure you've considered your set list (including input from the venue) and dress code before you start playing.

4.2 Try to talk to the audience a little in between numbers to help them relax and really enjoy your performance. Plan some of this in advance so you won't struggle for something to say.

4.3 Get the audience involved. Think about getting someone up on stage or having your singer walk out into the crowd as far as he can at some point.

4.4 Have a plan for if "disaster" strikes on stage.

4.5 Advertise the band name and a contact number on the stage.

4.6   Try to take someone along to each gig with a digital camera. Make sure they take plenty of pictures of ALL band members and some of the audience.

4.7   Make a note of any positive feedback you get on the night. You can use this on your future marketing efforts for the band.

4.8   ALWAYS try to book a follow-up gig (or more) after you come off stage.

4.9   Ask for your money.

5.   Do when the gigs are coming in

5.1   Aim to establish a string of venues where you play on a regular basis.

5.2   Design a basic newsletter format for your band. Use the newsletter to keep in touch with venues who initially said "No" to you or who promise to keep your details on file.

5.3   Keep adding material to your set lists so you will have something new for audiences at your regular venues.

5.4   Consider whether you're comfortable with being in the press on a regular basis. If so, draw up a list of likely publications and work on and send out regular news releases about your band's activities.

I wish you great success in all you do. Believe me, you **can** *make this happen!*

For the latest developments in how to get gigs and additional free monthly tips, go to:

http://www.gig-getter.com

Look out for this *NEW* gigging guide for semi-pro or amateur bands and musicians **from Gareth Bird**

ROUSE THE CROWD

How to interact with audiences for gigs they can't forget

- **Develop super-confidence onstage**

- **How to maximise positive crowd interaction at every gig – no matter how large (or small) the crowd**

- **3 key ways to make a crowd warm to you before you play a single note**

- **Secret ways to spot the most responsive crowd members in seconds- and how to use this to quickly build your overall crowd rapport**

- **11 sure-fire moments in every gig where you can build your crowd connection**

- **How to rouse any crowd even without an extrovert front person**

- **How to confidently talk to audiences in any situation onstage**

- **Tried and tested one-liners to woo every crowd**

Proven ways to develop your Stage Presence
For more info visit - http://www.gig-getter.com

Index

Advertising   13,30-31,60,63-65,
79-80,85,96,97-101
Appearance   14,21-22,71,73,82
Audience
-*Involvement*   19,76-77,79,81-82
- *Feedback*   22-23
-*Requests*   72,75,76
Availability   25-26,91,104
Aweber   73

Banter   13,15,17,72,77
Bio   49
Boss   20

Competition   12-13,16,29
Confidence   51-52
Covers   12,16,19-20,48
Crowd   71-73

Demo   43-46,49,50,59,61,
85-86, 95
Disaster   77
Dress   21-22,71,82-83

Email   35,65,66,67,73,105

Fairs   30
Festivals   30

Gig Diary   27-28,35-36,37,90-91
Goals   25

Hard Rock   7,83
Hotels   30,49, 71

Interaction   15

Material   15,19,20,29,44,47,
58-59,72,74-75,77
Medley   43-44
Myspace   44,65

Newsletter   61,81,103-107

Open mic   22
Organising   35,39-40,56
Original Material   12,17,19,48

Payment   26-27,59-61,
89-90
Phone   48,51-61,81,103
Photos/jpeg   47,64,67,81-83,
100,104,105,107
Posters   60,63-65,79,81,85
Practise   20-22,61
Press   61,65-67,97-101
Price   26-27,59-61
Private Function   31,71-72,79,95-96

Quotes   48,64,85-87,89,104

Repeat gigs   79,90-91,95

Selling   11,16,32,47,51-61
Set List   71-72,74-75
Strengths   14-16,43-44,74

Tascam   20

USP   16,59

Venue   40,53,59,63,71,83,
85,86,90,95-96,103
-Ads   13,65
-calling   35,52,61,103-107
-finding   29-32

Websites   29,49,73,105-106
-searches   12
Weddings   19,22,26,31,47,71,
72,79